D1564448

Essential Managerial Finance For Facilities Management

. . . articulating the value of facilities services in a language understood by the senior management and stakeholders

Steven Ee

Copyright © 2018 Steven Ee.

All rights reserved. No portion of this book may be reproduced or transmitted in any form or by any means – photocopy, scanning, or otherwise, without the prior permission of the author, except for inclusion of brief quotations in reviews or articles.

Essential Managerial Finance for Facilities Management

...articulating the value of facilities services in a language understood by the senior management and stakeholders

Author: Steven Ee
Website: www.stevenee.com
Email: steven@stevenee.com

ISBN-13: 978-1727760897
ISBN-10: 1727760891

Contents

Preface

Facilities Management (FM) exist to facilitate business operation success. However, there still some senior management have the misconception that facilities management as a "cost center" or a "liability". Thus, it is important for FM practitioners to be competent in some numerical skills and able to articulate their contribution in financial term.

Also as a financial steward, FM practitioner is responsible to make decisions that would best benefit its client or organization through managing its operations expenses and investing in the feasible new or facilities improvements initiatives.

The purpose of this book is to provide a guide to FM practitioners on how to be a good financial steward by demonstrating the ability to prioritize, manage, control and take responsibility for the outcomes. In doing well, facilities management is able to communicate the language understood by the senior management and be relied on as a trustworthy business partner.

This book is organized into 3 parts:

1. Budgeting for FM Workplan
2. Financial Benefit Analysis
3. Project Financial Evaluation

The key objectives of this book are to equip FM practitioners with the knowledge and skills on how to:

1. Prepare a budget for facilities management's workplan.

2. Perform Total Cost Analysis and Life Cycle Costing to assist in the decision making of facilities procurement or major repair or maintenance works;

3. Conduct a feasibility study for new facilities or initiative for facilities improvement;

This book tells you the essentials of communicating and articulating the expected facilities management performance deliverables in financial terms, a language that is understood well by the senior management.

It is the aim of this book that when you have finished reading, you will appreciate the need for FM practitioners to be ably equipped with the essential financial knowledge and skills to perform asset-based financial analysis, project financial evaluation and budgeting to build ties with the senior management and to obtain the financial resources for the planned workplan, with confidence. On your part, you will need to practice to be competent in it.

To your FM success!

Steven Ee

Website: www.Value-Based-FM.com
Email: steven@Value-Based-FM.com

Introduction

Essential Managerial Finance for Facilities Management

Introduction

Facilities management need to become more aware of the financial implications of our work upon the organizations' financial bottom-line. As FM practitioners, we have been entrusted to oversee the facilities and services of the organizations in accommodating and facilitating the business operations well and to enable the workplace to be safe, healthy, secure, and

FM practitioners must be good financial stewards

comfortable. The building and its services often represent a large investment for the organization and their running costs account for significant parts of the organization's annual expenditures.

An ethic of facilities management is to embody the responsibility of planning and management of the financial and available resources entrusted. That means FM practitioners are expected to make that capital and operating expenses' decisions that would best benefit their organizations and its stakeholders.

For FM practitioners to be regarded as good financial stewards, they need to be able to:

- Prioritise the facilities operations activities and services needs and wants;
- Conduct financial analysis for procurement and operations options;
- Budget for its planned annual and short-term Workplan;
- Monitor and report the progressive expenditures and demonstrate control of the variances;
- Identify, assess and manage risks.

Today's senior management tends to have strong business fundamental and less technical and functional expertise. They tend to be responsible for:

- long-term strategic plans,
- measuring performance, reporting the numbers to ensure that the functions that they are responsible for are aligned with the organization's strategic plans and objectives,
- continual value-creation and financial advantages.

To build ties with the senior management, FM practitioners need to know the business and the processes that they are supporting, learn the language of business and demonstrate in financial terms on how they support the organization's strategic plans.

So, what skills and financial knowledge do FM practitioners need?

- To make the right decisions in procuring new facilities, initiating facilities improvement, major repair, refurbishment and maintenance works?
- To compete with other functional departments for the limited financial resources?
- To build better ties with the senior management?
- To demonstrate that they are reliable and trustworthy as financial stewards?

All these and more are what you will learn in this book.

Let the learning begins . . . . .

Part 1:

Budgeting for FM Workplan

Budgeting for FM Workplan

"It is not difficult, just follow the same as previous years"

"Just mark-up 5% to last year figures"

"Waste of time – I got more urgent matter to attend"

"Just wait for Finance to tell us how much is allotted to us"

Budgeting is one activity in Facilities Management job scope that most FM practitioners would like to avoid. I have come across many practitioners telling me that they have neglected to budget because they are too busy with their wide jobs. Also, they do not see its importance as they assume it should be more or less the same as the previous year.

However if they overlook an asset is due for replacement, e.g., end of life for the chiller; and did not take into consideration the replacement cost during the budgeting planning, FM will have to seek the management for approval again for this capital expenditure. As the amount can be quite substantial, the organization may not have the ready cash flow to sponsor the costly emergency spending or willing to make changes to their financial plans. Also, an event like this could stall your operations and put a huge question mark on you efficiency as a department.

These experiences will cause management to have the misconception that FM is always asking for money and disrupting their financial plans. It will make future approval even harder as they will then be prejudices against FM. All these make seeking approval for capital expenditure an unpleasant and nerve-wracking process for FM practitioners.

Budgeting played an important role in determining how smooth or stressful FM practitioners' job will be. By not planning ahead and not analyzing past expenses, what should FM do when the budget is cut? Or the sudden failures or breakdowns?

FM will then have to juggle with the approved fund, sometimes in the midst of all the stress, critical facilities management activities may be overlooked and the recovery may be too expensive.

Learning Objectives:

This chapter serves as a guide for FM practitioners in the preparation of a budget for Facilities Management Work plan and how to go about monitoring the expenditures, keeping it within the approved budget.

---

1. FM Budgets

Budgets are concern about the organization's financial goals towards achieving its mission and vision. Traditionally, budgets are used to monitor progress, compare the actual performance against projected results, establish variances and take corrective actions. So it is a viable decision making and performance evaluation tool.

Besides the traditional use of budgets, they are also used for:

- Establish priorities and set targets in numerical terms
- Assign responsibilities and accountability to managers and give them the flexibility to run things their way (within the budget).
- Communicate targets from management to employees

Thus, in preparing a budget, be sure of how the targets will be achieved and have a strategy in place to chart the directions and actions to be carried out, within the budgets.

Normally, the facilities management function does not generate income. Even if they do generate income, it will not be significant enough to offset its expenses. This is one of the major reasons why senior management sees facilities management function a cost center. To change that misconception, FM should strive to be good financial steward and help organisation to maximise profitability and control scarce resources.

In preparing a budget, be sure of how the targets will be achieved and have a strategy in place to chart the directions and actions to be carried out, within the budgets.

The facilities management expenses consist of operating expenses (OPEX) and capital expenses (CAPEX). As such, some years there may be requests for huge funds for assets replacement. If these capital expenditures are not included in the budget, it may upset the overall organization financial goals as assets replacement projects are often of significant cost that counters the organization's efforts to maintain as much financial flexibility as possible.

FM Budget is Mission and Outcome-Based

FM Workplan is the planned facilities services intended for facilitating business operation success. FM Budget expresses the workplan in financial terms. This will enable the FM practitioner to plan the budget by focusing on activities rather than on costs. The purpose is to ensure that the facilities services supporting the organization's strategy and objectives are being funded and not overlooked.

Planning an activity-based budget will help the FM practitioners when negotiating with the management during the approval process. In the event there is a request to cut cost, it makes it easier for the management to decide as to

Plan the budget by focusing on activities rather than on costs

which services to reduce as the services are budgeted based on the outcome. E.g. Instead of cutting the budget across by 5%, management may decide to cut off "good to have" services – such as removing in-door plants, landscaping or the in-house office barista service.

Another advantage, in addition to the one mentioned above is that it makes prioritization and resource allocation much easier.

It also reduces the possibilities of overlooking maintenance of critical facilities. The senior management is also informed of the consequences of the cut in the budget, resulting in non-performance all the FM activities.

Mission: To facilitate business operations success			
Workplan	**Budgeting**	**Output**	**Outcome**
Structure (break down) according to Regions / Countries, Multiple or single sites, Hard or Soft services	To put a "price tag" on every workplan activities that incur cost	Facilities & Support Services • Building • Internal ground • External ground • Architecture • M&E • Support Services	• Building & their services, space, grounds, assets to be able to operate till their expected useful life • Facilities to operate at their optimum performance • Pleasant users experience • Reliable services • Safe, secure, comfortable & productive workplace • Optimised use of utilities and resources

Figure 1.1: Expressing FM Workplan into FM Budget

Importance of FM Budgeting

As mentioned above, FM Budget is an expression of FM workplan in financial terms. Any reduction or cut will significantly affect the workplan. Thus, it is important for FM practitioners to be proficient in the essential financial language as FM budgets are often being scrutinized by the senior management due to the fact that FM expenditures are significantly high, usually second after its organization's salaries.

Establish competency

Validate creditability and professionalism

Evaluating and monitoring operations

That being said, what is the importance of FM budgeting?

- ***Establish FM's competency in facilitating business operations***

  FM budgets that align itself with the organization's mission and policies, as well as taking into account of external factors such as environmental influences, legal compliance, establish FM's competency in facilitating the business operations.

17

As FM practitioners, one of our significant challenges has always been to convince the senior management to recognize FM functions as a strategic function. By aligning their services with the organization's mission and policies; it not only demonstrate that FM does facilitate organizations' business success, it also helps FM to push for their recognition.

- ***Validate FM creditability and professionalism***

  Transparency of details and prioritization of the requirements based on the risk or urgency with the aim to assist the senior management to make their decisions. This will help increase the creditability of facilities management and encourage senior management to trust the professional advice of FM.

- ***Tool for evaluating and monitoring actual operations***

  Since the budget is translated from the workplan, it can be used to monitor that all the planned activities are carried out (i.e. reviewing of the variance between the budget and actual expenses) and ensure the smooth operations of the business.

What makes a good FM budget?

As mentioned above, FM budget should align with itself with the organisations' mission and policies, FM budgets should contain capital expenditure (often referred to as CAPEX); routine operating expenses and taking into account of preventive maintenance too.

2. Capital Budget

Capital budgets are often facilities management plans for major facilities refurbishment, expansion, and replacement. Facilities management has to anticipate the needs for facilities to adapt to its needs for organizational workplace change.

ASSET REGISTER

FACILITIES CONDITION SURVEY

FACILITIES AUDIT

FIVE YEARS WORKPLAN

Being a good steward, Facilities management must also ensure compliance with the legal requirements, which usually incur costs to enable compliance so that the business operations need not be interrupted. E.g. Code on Barrier Free Access will require the construction of ramps to allow wheelchair users to move from one level to another and installation of toilet fittings for persons with disabilities.

Facilities systems and their components have their limited useful life. They will eventually need to be replaced or upgrade. In other words, any plan for works involving add-on, alterations to improve the facilities performance or new facilities that CONTRIBUTE VALUE to the organization are classified as CAPITAL BUDGET.

When preparing a capital budget, how and from where does FM get the data needed to aid the budget preparation? There are many sources of data that can come in handy when preparing a capital budget, here are a few considerations.

Considerations

* ASSET REGISTER – as the name suggests is a list of all the assets owned by the organization. It would have information on the cost, date of acquisition, quality, useful life, and also disposal. Normally we can get this list from the Accounts Department.

It is important for FM to have an updated Asset Register. Other information that FM may want to include in the register – such as the manufacturer, the warranty period, maintenance requirements and physical location.

- FACILITIES CONDITION SURVEY – an inspection, survey, and evaluation of the facilities and systems.

  Use:

  o *the facilities systems/component has deteriorated earlier than the expected useful life – Assets replacement*

  o *to detect defects or abnormal operating condition which may require corrective action such as repair, refurbishment or replacement*

- FACILITIES AUDIT – is a more comprehensive review of the facilities systems. It establishes the baseline information about the components, policies, and procedures of the facilities systems.

  Use:

- o *Determine the capacity if it is sufficient to serve the increased need/usage for the premise*

- o *Determine the performance of the aging facilities and its efficiency against the cost of replacement.*

- FIVE YEARS WORKPLAN – It is a list of projected facilities replacement for the next 5 years. It can be organised into the building elements such as structural, architectural, mechanical and electrical, internal space and external ground, see Table 2.1. or it can be a breakdown of the system as in Table 2.2.

  Use:

  - o *Prepare the senior management of the essential asset replacement cost. Also, by spreading out the replacement cost can help to reduce the financial burden and more efficient use of funds.*

  - • *Plan major projects into the annual plan (which may spread over more than 1 year), ensure that minimum interruption to business operations as seen in the below table 2.2 Five year plan for Cooling Water System replacement.*

Five Years Work plan

FM must have a plan for repairing and replacing assets that have exceeded their useful lifespan. Let's examine why facilities planning is so vital to FM success. Alan Lakein's statement, "Failing to plan is planning to fail" bears truth especially in facilities maintenance management.

Too many times, due to a lack of proper planning, FM is forced to maintain substandard equipment that has exceeded its useful life. FM usually lay the blame on the senior management, for not allocating the necessary funds necessary to properly maintain or replace the equipment. That may be true, however, there may be another side of the coin.

Perhaps FM did not give the senior management enough advance warning that the equipment needs to be replaced or a costly repair needs to be performed. Due to FM oversight in budgeting, it did not request adequate funding for the replacement. In such cases,

FM should also shoulder a share of the blame. Of course, it's sometimes difficult to accept blame, especially when others (management specifically) are such easy targets. A proactive maintenance mind-set begins at home.

The five year FM workplan is a tool that will help facilities management to keep track of your facilities useful life and major maintenance. Below Table 2.1 is a sample abstract of a five year plan based on the building elements.

Table 2.1: Sample abstract of a 5 year workplan

Building Element	RUL (Yrs)	Year Install	2019 '000	2020 '000	2021 '000	2022 '000	2023 '000	Comments
Structural								
Roof	4	2012				$23		
Painting	3	2017			$20			
External Ground								
Parking Area	2	2016		$4				Overlay rear parking area
Pavement	5	2012					$37	Patch pavement & Signage
Fence	3	2012			$9			
Internal Space:								
Carpet	2	2015		$7				
Painting	2	2015		$5				Conference room & Office area
M & E								
Door Access	NA		$12					New installation for block 2

RUL – remaining useful life

Table 2.2: 5-Year Workplan Plan for Cooling Water System Replacement

Systems & Equipment	RUL	5-Year Budgeting Plan					
		2019 '000	2020 '000	2021 '000	2022 '000	2023 '000	2024 '000
1. Cooling Water System							
1.1 Cooling Tower 1	2		$200				
1.2 Cooling Tower 2	3			$200			
1.3 Cooling Water Pump 1	2		$5				
1.4 Cooling Water Pump 2	3			$5			
1.5 Chemical Dosing System	5					$2.5	

The beauty of this simple format is its ability to quickly communicate facilities services and their costs and date of scheduled replacement.

Without a plan facilities management will be stuck in a reactive mode, unable to control the time, the resources and the budget. For FM practitioners wishing to become more proactive, a five-year facilities management workplan is a must!

3. Operating Budget

The operating budget besides reflecting the operational activities, such as utilities, fire protection, security operation, cleaning and etc, it also encompasses routine maintenance and minor repairs, including the upkeep of facilities systems so that it can realize its estimated useful life and performance at its optimal level.

Measure Performance

Highlight critical issues

Predict cash flow

Maintenance will include periodic testing and inspection, adjustment, lubrication and cleaning of equipment that are included in the facilities management workplan.In other words, operating budget is used for the day-to-day running of FM operations.

Operating budget helps FM to:

- Measure performance against projected plans
- Draw the attention of senior management to areas that need urgent and continual attention.
- Predict cash flows

Operating budget is usually prepared annually, based on the estimated expenses associated with the Facilities Management Workplan for the year. See figure 3.1, Facilities Management Workplan Structure. It comprises of the facilities services, also known as the hard services, and support services, also known as the soft services.

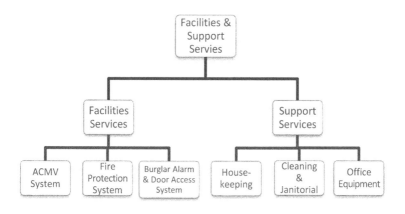

Figure 3.1: Facilities Management Workplan Structure

The services are then organized into the respective facilities systems and the services. See figure 3.2, Budgeting for Cooling Water System Maintenance, as part of the maintenance of Air conditioning and Mechanical Ventilation system. It presents the indicated costs of maintenance for the Colling Water System's components and planned expenditures for the year.

Activity	Annual Total ($)	Jan	Feb	Mar	Apr	May	Jun	Jul	Aug	Sep	Oct	Nov	Dec
Cooling Towers	8,000			2,000			2,000			2,000			2,000
Cooling Water Pumps	3,600	300	300	300	300	300	300	300	300	300	300	300	300
Chemical Water Treatmen	9,600	800	800	800	800	800	800	800	800	800	800	800	800
Electrical Supply	3,000						1,500						1,500
Water Supply	2,000												2,000

Figure 3.2: Budgeting for Cooling Water System Maintenance

The same way that Cooling Water System Maintenance was budgeted for as part of ACMV System, components of every other facilities system must be budget for as well. For instance, Fire Detection systems should be budgeted for under the Fire Protection System, and so on.

Besides budgeting for components of the various systems and services, operating budget should also capture overhead costs of the day to day running of FM services.

See figure 3.3, Overhead Budgeting Preparation illustrates the presentation of the personnel costs for the respective services and the categories of where the personnel is being deployed.

Item	Current Year 2018	New Year 2019	Reason
Contract Staff	148,000	153,920	4% company pay increase
Cleaning	330,000	330,000	Remain unchanged
Security	174,740	180,000	3% contract increased

Figure 3.3: Overhead Budgeting Preparation

Having a sound knowledge on how to set estimates for the respective facilities services will enable you to have a feel of the expected costs should your facilities management function decides to adopt Managing Contractor or Total Facilities Management outsourcing approach.

4. Chart of Accounts

It is a listing of all accounts used in organizations' general ledger for recording and organizing financial transactions. See figure 4.1 Chart of Accounts, an example of an organization structure of the Chart of Accounts. It is organized into major categories such as asset, liabilities, equity, revenue, and expense.

The accounts relevant to a Facilities Management function, within an organisation, are mostly classified under the Assets and Expenses categories. Know that the accounts can be added to suit the facilities management needs to better organize the financial transactions and charge expenses to the relevant departments.

Accountability

Maintenance Planning

Capital Budgeting

Monitoring of Expenses

Distribution of Expenses

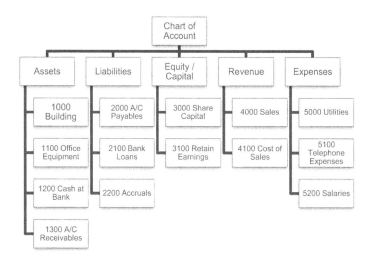

Figure 4.1: Chart of Accounts

Purpose or use for Chart of Accounts to FM.

For the assets category:

- ACCOUNTABILITY - it helps facilities management to keep track of assets that are under their care. In addition, It helps to ensure that no assets are overlooked when FM schedules assets maintenance.

- MAINTENANCE PLANNING – if the asset is near its end of life (fully depreciated i.e. zero book value), to ensure efficiency, FM should consider a replacement of assets instead of continuing the maintenance.

- CAPITAL BUDGETING – when the asset is fully depreciated, a request for replacement is easier to justify than an asset that still has book value.

For the expenses category:

- MONITORING OF EXPENSES – Instead of listing all servicing expenses under the repair and maintenance account, FM can further break them down to planned and unplanned maintenance. It will enable FM to monitor the unplanned maintenance trend and ease of investigation.

- DISTRIBUTION OF EXPENSES – If there are accounts for the expenses of each department or functions, FM should allocate and charge back the expenses to the relevant departments or functions. It will help to spread out the cost of facilities services and also justify the spending by FM.

If you are new or do not have access to the chart of accounts, you may allocate your facilities management costs or expenses to the functions or services such as:

- business units or functions;

- specific facilities systems and projects;

- resources eg. Internal contractors (general overheads), professionals, spares, consumables, tools, equipment, and services to the FM function.

- scope, such as:

  o Capital projects, for new, overhauled and replaced systems, additions and alterations building works, etc.

  o Preventive maintenance

  o Contingencies funds

  o Festive decorations eg. New Year, Christmas, Anniversary, etc.

Having done that, work with the finance and request the accounts code to be created for the above. It will be useful for reporting and monitoring of expenditure.

5. Planning Cycles

In this section, we are going to look at the FM budget planning cycle and the best approaches to adopt at each stage of the process.

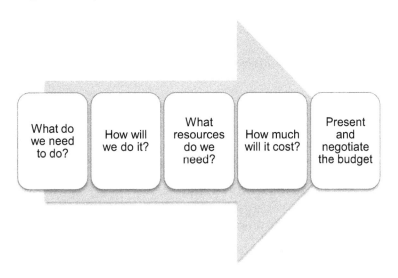

Figure 5.1: FM Budget Planning Cycle

What do we need to do?

- Know what you have – Asset Register

    o   If Asset Register is not available, request for the Chart of Accounts from the Accounts Department.

o What are their conditions – Condition Survey

o Group the facilities system by the criticality and essentials. Every business is different, of course, so necessary or critical systems for one organization are not always essential or critical for another. The following sequence helps to prioritize the facilities services:

  ❖ Identify the organization's business operations processes;

  ❖ Identify the facilities services serving those operations, the respective functions and their activities;

  ❖ Identify the critical business operations;

  ❖ Identify the facilities services serving those critical business operations.

  ❖ Prioritise the facilities services according to the risks, arising from the failure of the facilities services.

• Know your organization strategic objectives

o Goals and KPI should be translated from organization objectives. This will ensure that the efforts of facilities team are contributing positively towards achieving the organisation's strategic objective.

- Know your FM objectives – Facilities Management Workplan

How will we do it?

- Know what you need to do to ensure the facilities are operating at peak performance

- Know what barriers that prevent you from achieving the objectives

- Know the plan for each facility system:

  o Is there a change of use for the facility?

  o How will the organization's strategic objectives impact the use or need for the facility systems?

What resources do we need?

- Do a breakdown structure of facilities services.

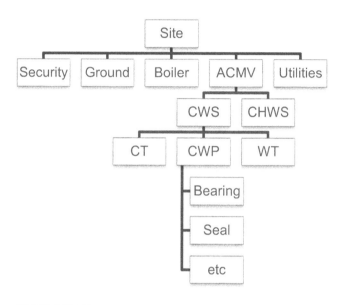

ACMV	Air-Conditioning and Mechanical Ventilation	CT	Cooling Tower
CWS	Cooling Water System	CWP	Cooling Water Pump
CHWS	Chilled Water System	WT	Water Treatment

Figure 5.2: Breakdown structure of FM services

- With the work breakdown structure, we can then estimate the financial resource required is based on the total cost of labors, materials, consumables, parts for replacement for the planned maintenance works. In turn, the total costs shall be charged to the functional department cost center, that uses the facilities services as shown in the diagram below.

Figure 5.3: Using the Breakdown Structure to estimate costing

How much will it cost?

- Assign a reasonable and practical cost to each line item of the work
  - ○ Request For Quotations, Request For Information
  - ○ Inflation rate and the discounted rate could be obtained from the organization's Finance department. If it is not available internally, FM can use the published Consumer Price Index (CPI) by the Statistics Department

- Sum up the costing

- Identify the potential savings that could be implemented

Present and negotiate the budget.

Once you are done with budget preparation, the next phase is budget presentation and negotiation. Usually, senior management often scrutinizes FM budget critically. In other words, FM is commonly held to a higher standard of justification than core business functions. The reason being that, FM functions are deemed as overheads (cost center, a function that does not generate revenue), so, senior management does try to cut costs emanating from this department. Also, facilities projects often involve high capital and operating costs and long-term financial commitments.

Strategy to convince them of the desirability, feasibility and cost effectiveness

Budget presentation and negotiation is a crucial strategy in getting the buy-in from the decision makers, convincing them of the desirability, feasibility, and cost-effectiveness of the programme. A well-structured presentation will put you in a good negotiating position to ensure your proposed budget is approved.

The below figure, Presentation of the proposed FM Budget, illustrates the five steps sequence in presentation.

Your presentation should be well organized and divided into various slides

On the first presentation slide, present the organization's mission and objectives to demonstrate the awareness to the senior management that the FM services are planned to achieve them through its set objectives and the Five Year Plan.

Figure 5.4: Presentation of the proposed FM Budget

The second slide is to present the significantly proposed budgets intended to support the objectives.

The third slide presents the overview of the proposed FM budget, contributing to the recipients of the services.

The fourth slide presents the past year(s) FM performance and their expenditures emphasizing the value contributions to the organisation;

The final slide is intended to demonstrate that the FM Workplan is well thought to ensure effective delivery of to meet the demands, objectives and targets of the organisation.

FM has to dedicate time to budget presentation and negotiation. A good fight must be put up because if FM budget is cut, it is going to tell on the performance of the department, and the senior management's general perception of the department will continue to go down.

Therefore, preparing a good budget is not where the job of the FM ends, ensuring that the budget is accepted with only minor alternations should be the primary aim of the FM.

Follow up the rejected proposed budget

When faced with the challenge of cutting costs, response in a manner that "FM do not manage costs, we manage activities" – cutting costs means doing less activities or finding

Identify those functions that are critical to the realisation of the overall business objectives of the organisation

cheaper ways of doing the activities, which may affect the delivery of the organisation's objectives and the functional needs for facilities services.

FM has to persevere in their efforts to make senior management see how cutting costs is going to affect the functions of the department and stall the realisation of the overall goals and mission of the organisation.

Unless all efforts to get the buy-in for the needed budget fails (based on top-down allocated budget), FM practitioners just need prioritise the resources and focus the expenditures on the activities that are most important in facilitating the organisation's business operations.

What are the best ways to prioritise functions and resources? FM has to go back to the drawing board and use a green/yellow/red system to identify those functions that are critical to the realisation of the overall business objectives of the organisation.

Mandatory tasks such as in compliance with workplace safety and health should be designated as red. This sends a signal to the senior management that fund for these kinds of tasks must be a top priority.

Less urgent matters should be designated as yellow while the "nice-to-haves" should be designated green and pushed to the bottom of the budget list. Using this kind of a destination system makes it easier for the FM to justify the inclusion of certain tasks in the budget.

Upon completing the adjustments to the proposed budgets, present to the senior management on the reduced or removed proposed budgets stating the effects and consequence of the adjustments, if any, or highlight the alternate services to the earlier proposal.

Senior management often tend to reduce the proposed budgets because they felt that FM tends to produce budgets based on the previous year's actual expenditures with a few tweaks. Very often, they will be tempted to "pad" their budget in preparation of their proposed budget being cut. This leads to repeated budget processes where budgets are padded, then cut by increasing amounts each year.

Allocate Approved Budget to Workplan

Upon securing the allocated approved budget, next, prepare to allocate the planned expenditures to the Workplan's activities. This is the area where the FM has to show its accountability and ability to be a good financial steward.

Allocation of the approved budget should be done in such a manner that planned promises are delivered. Budget allocation should also be done so that extra costs are not incurred in the overall implementation of the budget.

If FM does not allocate an approved budget to workplan, then FM should expect some resistance from the senior management when next it is time for budget presentation and negotiation.

6. Expenditures Monitoring

After the budgeting has been approved and allocated to workplan, next comes monitoring the progress of expenditures against the approved budgets.

The approved budget serves as a yardstick to monitor and measure the achievement of the Workplan activities and to assess the difference between the actual expenses and allocated budgets for the activities.

The key purpose is to track spending that are over the allocated budgets so that corrective action may be taken for their variances.

FM expenditures are usually tracked at least monthly and to report to its superior or the senior management to communicate the reasons for variances, such as; changes to the planned activities and the new cost baseline set for the future (due to costs of legislative compliance, change of workplace requirement, etc.).

In doing so, FM is demonstrating accountability and pro-activeness in reporting the measurements and the actions taken to close those variances.

Presenting the Expenditure Report

Regular expenditures reports should be prepared and presented to the senior management by FM. These should be in the same format as the budgets and should give the figures for the actual results alongside the equivalent budget figures.

Variances should also be given and it is usual to give the figures for the period (perhaps a month) and for the year to date as well. See figure 7.1, Accumulative Expenditures Monitoring. It is an example of a formate that illustrates the spending against the planned budget and to indicate the variances, if any.

Items	June Month			June YTD		
	Budget ($)	Actual ($)	Variance ($)	Budget ($)	Actual ($)	Variance ($)

Figure 6.1: Accumulative Expenditures Monitoring

The format of the FM expenditures would usually contain the following information:

- Monthly and cumulative actual expenditure; and
- Monthly and cumulative variance of expenditure against budget.

The variances are usually expressed in monetary terms, but it is sometimes it may be expressed in percentages as well. If it is done in percentages, you should consider the size of the figures. An overrun of $50 on a budget of $100 is a 50% adverse variance, though it is insignificant. On the other hand, an overrun of $50 on a budget of $10,000 is just a 0.5% adverse variance.

Budget variance reports need careful interpretation. There are no absolute rules for the format of budget variance reports, so you should have one that is simple and suits your needs.

Conclusion

FM practitioners should appreciate the budgeting process of their organisation. The budget is an indication of how the organisation works, what it cares about, and what direction it is pursuing. A review of budgetary decisions will also reveal whether or not a particular business line is likely to warrant new or continued investment in facilities and their services.

For an FM budget to be effective, it needs to be flexible to adapt to the organisation's business performance and strategies. When business performs well, it is an opportunity to perform the delayed major refurbishment and replacements. When business is performing well despite of economic turbulence, FM should take

For an FM budget to be effective, it needs to be flexible to adapt to the organisation's business performance and strategies

the opportunity of the market competition to carry out major improvement works, additions and alterations to enhance the workplace to be more productive in supporting the business operations.

Whereas, when business performance is not performing well, that is when facilities management needs to perform resource prioritisation and be frugal on its workplan.

FM has to demonstrate as good stewards of the funding allocated to FM. It needs to demonstrate that facilities services support organisation's strategy and its objectives. It should show how facilities services will operate, in supporting to each of its internal customers reflecting the "demand for facilities services" and "Supply at a cost".

When preparing the budget, be transparent and involve your team members. Get the facilities systems and support services responsible persons to be involved in setting up the forecast. Involve your team and helping them to understand the budgeting process. That is to create a sense of shared ownership of the budget for their areas of services and to manage their expenses.

Part 2:

Financial Benefit Analysis

Financial Benefit Analysis

"What has finance got to do with FM?"

"Our roles are to operate and maintain the building and its services."

"We do not do numbers. That's the Finance department and senior management job".

Most FM practitioners often echo these common responses. However, the truth remains that FM practitioners also have some financial analysis to do as well.

If FM practitioners are not able to demonstrate its importance in contributing to their organizations' financial bottom-line, they are not likely able to rise to the strategic level or be considered as a business partner.

Learning Objectives:

In Financial Benefit Analysis, you will learn Total Cost Analysis and Life Cycle Costing, in considering the costs for the life of the facility asset's options, in making sound procurement decisions.

7. Tactical versus Strategic Decision Making

Traditionally, the role of facilities management is one of a tactical nature, meaning it makes decisions that have immediate consequences. If we choose to repair a leaking roof or if we choose to defer changing of a light bulb, the organisation experiences the immediate benefits or consequences of these decisions. However, it is important to look beyond the tactical nature of facilities management services and examine the strategic nature of the practice.

Making tactical decisions reflect the nature of short-term considerations which often result in fire-fighting, fixing defects and failure and then move on to the next problem and the cycle repeats. Thus, it is important for FM practitioners to put on the strategic-thinking hat, considering the long-term consequences. Although the decision to choose a higher priced option may seem not to make financial sense, in the long run, it makes better financial sense.

It is understood that FM practitioners have been known to be involved in spontaneous decision-making; however, if FM is ever going to be competing with the other departments, especially in regards to allocation of funds, FM practitioners have to start thinking strategically.

8. The Gatekeeper

The term "gatekeeper" is used to describe the individual that controls the resources, particularly the financial resource, needed by facilities management for its operations and in delivering the workplan's activities. Thus, FM practitioners need to know who the gatekeepers are and their role.

The gatekeeper could be your boss, your bosses' boss, the finance staff – whoever. This gatekeeper is responsible for allocating out a limited pool of money to various functional departments. You are in competition with them who have their hands out for the money and some of these have some legitimate needs just like yourselves, so how do you stand out.

Unlike the favored "profit centers", such as the sales department or the manufacturing department, FM department who does not directly contribute to the revenue, is perceived as a "cost center" and liability to the organization. So in a competition for the limited funds, most of the time, FM will lose out unless it is back up by legal requirements or absolute necessity.

So let's understand the reality of how the gatekeeper disburses your organization's funds. First, we must understand that there is a limited amount of funds are available to meet the many needs. We are in direct competition with other departments, including those considered profit centers.

For instance, suppose the manufacturing department, a profit center, has requested a new conveying system that speeds up the manufacturing process thereby increasing the revenue of the organization by 25%. The cost of this system is $257,000. The sales department, a profit center, is requesting a server upgrade and new computers for the salespeople at a cost of $177,000. FM department, a "cost center", is requesting $198,000 for replacement of carpet, paint and the roofs.

Do you see the competition for your organization's dollars? Can you predict how the gatekeeper will disburse the funds? Yes, FM department will likely be getting the crumbs only.

Due to the harsh competition, FM practitioners must learn to be more persuasive when dealing with the gatekeeper. You have to make a case to justify for the funding. You must be able to demonstrate the financial value contribution to the organization for procuring new facilities or when initiating facilities improvement. You will need to have a detailed plan, 5-Year Workplan, for your facilities. The requests, by FM department, must be backed up by benchmarked life spans and costs.

Also when requesting funds from the gatekeeper, you will likely be pressured to choose the low bidder. For this reason, you must understand and be able to articulate the difference between cost and price.

9. Understand the Difference Between Price and Cost

Often, management makes purchasing decisions based on the price of the asset. When comparing options, management would usually choose the option that is the least expensive. If Option 1 is priced at $ 150,000, Option 2 is priced at $ 180,000 and Option 3 is priced at $ 200,000, likely Option 1 will be selected. You probably know that the decision may not be the best choice. In facilities operations, it is concerned with the long-range "strategic" evaluation rather than based on short-term.

It is important for FM practitioners to understand the difference between cost and price. The two terms may sound similar but actually, they have very different meanings.

Price is the initial investment necessary to acquire an asset. It is often an area where the senior management tends to get excited about if they perceive the price to be too high or if an option exists at a lower price.

Cost, however includes not just the initial investment but all other expenses associated with owning that asset; for instance, utility and maintenance costs.

It describes the total financial responsibility of ownership. This being the case, cost should always be the benchmark, not just price, particularly when examining the "low bid".

Cost includes all the expenses associated with owning that asset

Figure 9.1 illustrates the impact of price and cost on the value of a facility asset.

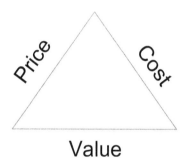

Figure 9.1: Price and Cost

When making facilities-based financial analysis, there are generally two options:

1.　Total Cost Analysis (TCA)
2.　Life Cycle Costing (LCC)

10. Total Cost Analysis (TCA)

In today's world where there is an ever-increasing demand for improved quality of facilities services, FM needs to ensure that the facilities services are reliable and available, especially when they are serving the critical functions. To achieve the high performance of the facilities services, routine preventative and predictive maintenance must be factored in together with the cost to operate the facilities, i.e. utilities (electricity, water, and gas), and labor.

A Total Cost Analysis is a method that allows you to compare the true costs of various options, even if the options have different useful life spans and maintenance costs.

The Total Cost Analysis is an excellent tool for understanding the long-term impact of varied price points, including lease/buy decisions.

For instance, let's suppose you had two bids for a facility equipment.

- Option 1 @ $ 200,000
- Option 2 @ $ 130,000

Based on "traditional" reasoning, Option 2 would be selected, as it is priced lower. That would be a decision based on "price" (initial investment) instead of "cost" (includes everything).

Now, here is more information about the two bids:

	Initial Price	ULS	Annual Maint. Costs	Annual Energy Costs	Total Cost
Option 1	$200,000	10	$1,500	$1,000	$225,000
Option 2	$130,000	5	$1,000	$1,000	$140,000

TC = IP + (AMC + AEC x ULS)
TC = Total Cost
IP = Initial Price
AMC = Annual Maintenance Costs
AEC = Annual Energy Costs
ULS = Useful Life Span

Figure 10.1: Total cost of two bids

Based on this information, maybe the "Option 2" is the right option. However, we must look at the wildcard - "Useful Lifespan" for each option. It would be unfair to compare an asset priced at $200,000 that last ten years to an asset priced at $130,000 but lasting only five years based on initial purchase price or even the total cost.

When comparing different options with different lifespans, we must extrapolate the costs on a per year basis for each option. If we desire to create an equitable comparison, the formula it would look like this:

TC Annualized = TC / ULS

	Initial Price	ULS	Annual Maint. Costs	Annual Energy Costs	Total Cost	Total Cost Annualized
Option 1	$200,000	10	$1,500	$1,000	$225,000	$22,500
Option 2	$130,000	5	$1,000	$1,000	$140,000	$28,000

Figure10.2: Total Cost Annualized

Based on the comparison table above, you'll notice that the low bid option 2 is of a higher cost on a per year basis.

Total Cost Analysis works well when evaluating multiple options with different equipment operating cost and life spans.

In this example, the better choice would be Option 1. Although Option 1 has a greater initial price, the cost over the life of the asset is $ 5,500 lesser per year. This may be a very simplistic example, but it reinforces the value of performing Total Cost Analysis for all purchases.

11. Life Cycle Costing

Another method of financial analysis is the Life Cycle Costing, LCC. This analysis is different from the total cost analysis in one very specific and important area. The LCC method includes the concept of the time value of money. It describes future costs in terms of today's dollar or present value.

We understand the concept of a dollar today has more value than a dollar next year. The future value of a dollar erodes each year due to inflation and lost opportunity to earn interest - "opportunity cost". These dynamics are considered when we perform a life cycle cost analysis.

This may seem like an unnecessary step that adds little value to our decision-making process, but the opposite is actually true. These are the methods financial and purchasing managers use to make important financial decisions. If we can learn to "speak their language" and present to them options in a way they understand, we will have higher chance of succeeding in persuading the management to make the right decision, even if it is initially the more expensive decision.

In the following example, we will evaluate two options, each with different initial purchase prices, useful lifespans, maintenance costs and energy costs. We will attempt to make a sound financial decision based on the future cost of the asset.

Example 1:

Air-Conditioning System	Packaged Unit	Centralised System
Life Span	12 yrs	20 yrs
Capital Cost	$150,000	$200,000
Maintenance Cost (Annual)	$8,000	$15,000
Energy Cost (Annual)	$18,000	$23,000

The discount rate is normally the organizations calculated the weighted average cost of capital (WACC) and use for budgeting a new project. The Finance department will be able to provide the discount rate as well as the inflation rate.

In this example, it will be assume at 8%

Figure 11.1: Life Cycle Costing Calculation for Packaged Unit

Packaged Unit			Discount Rate: 8%		
Time Period	Initial Cost	Maint. Cost	Energy Cost	PV Factor	Present Value
	(a)	(b)	(c)	(d)	(a+b+c) x d
0	$ 150,000			1	$ 150,000
1		$ 8,000	$ 18,000	0.9259	$ 24,073
2		$ 8,000	$ 18,000	0.8573	$ 22,290
3		$ 8,000	$ 18,000	0.7938	$ 20,639
4		$ 8,000	$ 18,000	0.7350	$ 19,110
5		$ 8,000	$ 18,000	0.6806	$ 17,696
6		$ 8,000	$ 18,000	0.6302	$ 16,385
7		$ 8,000	$ 18,000	0.5835	$ 15,171
8		$ 8,000	$ 18,000	0.5403	$ 14,048
9		$ 8,000	$ 18,000	0.5002	$ 13,005
10		$ 8,000	$ 18,000	0.4632	$ 12,043
11		$ 8,000	$ 18,000	0.4289	$ 11,151
12		$ 8,000	$ 18,000	0.3971	$ 10,325
	$ 150,000	$96,000	$216,000		$345,936

The table above represents the life cycle costing of packaged unit. The last column reflects the total costs for each future time period in present value or worth. That number is derived using an annually decreasing factor (PV Factor).

The PV factor is a discount factor, which establishes future costs in today's dollars.

PV Factor = 1/(1+i)n   *i = interest rate; n = time period*

Figure 11.2: Life Cycle Costing Calculation for Centralized System

	Centralized System			Discount Rate: 8%	
Time Period	Initial Cost	Maint. Cost	Energy Cost	PV Factor	Present Value
	(a)	(b)	(c)	(d)	(a+b+c) x d
0	$ 200,000			1	$ 200,000
1		$ 15,000	$ 23,000	0.9259	$ 35,845
2		$ 15,000	$ 23,000	0.8573	$ 32,577
3		$ 15,000	$ 23,000	0.7938	$ 30,164
4		$ 15,000	$ 23,000	0.7350	$ 27,930
5		$ 15,000	$ 23,000	0.6806	$ 25,863
6		$ 15,000	$ 23,000	0.6302	$ 23,948
7		$ 15,000	$ 23,000	0.5835	$ 22,173
8		$ 15,000	$ 23,000	0.5403	$ 20,531
9		$ 15,000	$ 23,000	0.5002	$ 19,008
10		$ 15,000	$ 23,000	0.4632	$ 17,602
11		$ 15,000	$ 23,000	0.4289	$ 16,298
12		$ 15,000	$ 23,000	0.3971	$ 15,090
13		$ 15,000	$ 23,000	0.3677	$ 13,973
14		$ 15,000	$ 23,000	0.3405	$ 12,939
15		$ 15,000	$ 23,000	0.3152	$ 11,978
16		$ 15,000	$ 23,000	0.2919	$ 11,092
17		$ 15,000	$ 23,000	0.2703	$ 10,271
18		$ 15,000	$ 23,000	0.2502	$ 9,508
19		$ 15,000	$ 23,000	0.2317	$ 8,805
20		$ 15,000	$ 23,000	0.2145	$ 8,151
	$ 200,000	$300,000	$460,000		$573,084

Presentation of Life Cycle Costing

Option	Packaged Unit	Centralized System
Initial Cost	$150,000	$200,000
Maintenance Cost (Annual)	$ 8,000	$ 15,000
Energy Cost (Annual)	$ 18,000	$ 23,000
Useful Life	12	20
PV Total Cost	$345,936	$573,084
PV Total Cost Annualized	$ 28,828	$ 28,654

When examining these two options, although Centralized System requires a higher initial cash outlay and cost slightly more in annual maintenance and energy consumption; it is actually less expensive over the term of its useful life. The annualized present value of the total cost is $28,654 compares with the annualized present value of the total cost of packaged unit $28,828. The slight saving will be $174 (in today's dollars) per year.

Example 2:

Floor Finishes	Teak Parquet Wood	Polished Marble
Life Span	12 yrs	>20 yrs
Capital Cost	$576,000	$720,000
Maintenance Cost (Annual)	$20,000	$25,000
Ave, Area Coverage	3,600m²	3,600m²

Figure 11.3: Life Cycle Costing Calculation for Teak Parquet Wood

Teak Parquet Wood			Discount Rate: 8%	
Time Period	Initial Cost	Maint. Cost	PV Factor	Present Value
	(a)	(b)	(d)	(a+b+c) x d
0	$ 576,000		1	$ 576,000
1		$ 20,000	0.9259	$ 18,518
2		$ 20,000	0.8573	$ 17,146
3		$ 20,000	0.7938	$ 15,876
4		$ 20,000	0.7350	$ 14,700
5		$ 20,000	0.6806	$ 13,612
6		$ 20,000	0.6302	$ 12,604
7		$ 20,000	0.5835	$ 11,670
8		$ 20,000	0.5403	$ 10,806
9		$ 20,000	0.5002	$ 10,004
10		$ 20,000	0.4632	$ 9,264
11		$ 20,000	0.4289	$ 8,578
12		$ 20,000	0.3971	$ 7,942
	$ 576,000	**$240,000**		**$ 726,720**

Figure 11.4: Life Cycle Costing Calculation for Polished Marble

	Polished Marble		Discount Rate: 8%	
Time Period	Initial Cost	Maint. Cost	PV Factor	Present Value
	(a)	(b)	(d)	(a+b+c) x d
0	$ 720,000		1	$ 720,000
1		$ 25,000	0.9259	$ 23,148
2		$ 25,000	0.8573	$ 21,433
3		$ 25,000	0.7938	$ 19,845
4		$ 25,000	0.7350	$ 18,375
5		$ 25,000	0.6806	$ 17,015
6		$ 25,000	0.6302	$ 15,755
7		$ 25,000	0.5835	$ 14,588
8		$ 25,000	0.5403	$ 13,508
9		$ 25,000	0.5002	$ 12,505
10		$ 25,000	0.4632	$ 11,580
11		$ 25,000	0.4289	$ 10,723
12		$ 25,000	0.3971	$ 9,928
13		$ 25,000	0.3677	$ 9,193
14		$ 25,000	0.3405	$ 8,513
15		$ 25,000	0.3152	$ 7,880
16		$ 25,000	0.2919	$ 7,298
17		$ 25,000	0.2703	$ 6,758
18		$ 25,000	0.2502	$ 6,255
19		$ 25,000	0.2317	$ 5,793
20		$ 25,000	0.2145	$ 5,363
	$ 720,000	**$375,000**		**$ 965,450**

Presentation of Life Cycle Costing

Option	Teak Parquet Wood	Polished Marble
Initial Cost	$576,000	$720,000
Maintenance Cost (Annual)	$ 20,000	$ 25,000
Useful Life	12	20
PV Total Cost	$726,720	$965,450
PV Total Cost Annualized	$ 60,560	$ 48,273

The polished marble option has a higher initial price, but longer useful life span. Thus if we annualized the present value of the total cost, the saving is ($60,560 - $ 48,273) = $12,287.

Armed with this information, we can make informed economic decisions that actually save substantial amounts of money.

Life Cycle Costing enables comparison of different options with different life spans. It is able to provide the senior management with an equitable comparison of these options using today's present value of money.

Conclusion

Instead of investing twenty hours trying to save three cents on a light bulb or spending time squeezing dollars from your already profit poor janitorial vendor, why not try using life cycle costing as a method to improve the bottom line?

If we can change our attitudes about purchasing facilities assets and view them as they actually are - financial investments, we will make better decisions. We will begin to treat these investments as an organization would view any other important investment such as hiring personnel or expansion into other territories. The resistance we typically receive from the senior management will dissipate as we become more adept at highlighting the long-term strategic benefits of an initially more expensive purchase.

We may not have an MBA, and we may feel that numbers are not our strong suit, but we do have a responsibility as FM Practitioners to make good financial decisions. These financial analysis methods will help you to make (and explain) better financial decisions.

Part 3

Project Financial Evaluation

Project Financial Evaluation

Would the company accept all the proposals for improvements?

What are the criteria for approval?

Do all proposals with a positive net present value will be accepted?

What if the available funds are limited? How will the monies be allocated?

How to articulate the return on investment for our prjects?

FM does not generate revenue, so how to justify?

The above are questions often asked by FM practitioners. Their frustrations are real as facilities projects cannot finance itself, and often the investment amounts required is huge. The situation is made worst if FM practitioner cannot justify the return on investment or state why management should allocate such huge funds to FM.

FM department, like others, has to compete for the limited resources available. The perception of the FM function being a cost center and FM practitioners who are not adept in persuasion skills often will lose out in the competition.

To compete well for the limited resources available, FM practitioners have to be equipped with the knowledge on the criteria to be satisfied in order to gain the senior management's approval.

FM practitioners must be able to present in a way to impress upon to the senior management that a dollar saved has the same or even more impact on the company's "bottom line" as those revenue-enhancing proposals.

Learning Objectives:

Conduct feasibility for new or facilities improvement initiatives with the aim to win funds for the proposed projects.

---

12. Project Feasibility

Feasibility study often takes place during the inception or conceptual of an idea or proposed project.

The aims of conducting feasibility study are to:

- Explore possible options for implementing the project
- Achieve a clear understanding of the potential issues involved
- Produce sufficient information for ranking of options
- Obtain a clear plan for the entire project

The feasibility study enables evaluation of:

- Cost justification
- Alternative means
- Risk that may be involved
- Goal and objectives of the initiative.

The end result of the feasibility study is a management decision on whether to accept or reject the proposed project.

13. Decision Making Tools

Decision-making tools are means to enable management to prioritize and decide on resources allocation. The gatekeepers, such as the senior management and Chief Financial Officer, are likely to have in-place a variety of tools to evaluate the competing requests for financial funding, to guide the "go or no-go" decision on those competing requirements and/or to prioritize the requirements.

Commonly, organizations have used one of the following financial decision-making tools to determine the feasibilities of the proposed projects

- Payback or break even
- Return on Investment (ROI)
- Internal Rate of Return (IRR)
- Net Present Value (NPV)
- Benefit to Cost Ratio (B/C)

The table below contrasts characteristics of the three major capital budgeting techniques most used by business today.

- "Yes" means the technique meets the criterion stated

- "No" means that it does not

- All it takes is one "No" to indicate that under certain circumstances, the technique may be inferior.

Figure 13.1: Qualities of Capital Budgeting Techniques

	Payback	NPV	ROI
Considers time value of $	No	Yes	No
Considers all cash flows	No	Yes	Yes
Considers risk	Yes	No	Yes
Considers return	No	Yes	Yes
Easy to understand	Yes	Yes	Yes
Easy to compute	Yes	No	Yes
Maximize the value of the firm	No	Yes	Yes
Considers project's profitability	No	Yes	Yes

In addition to the above considerations that are appropriate to FM are Total Cost Analysis and Life Cycle Costing which are explained the earlier chapter in Part 2 "Facilities-Based Financial Analysis".

14. Project Selection

FM strategic projects are those initiatives or projects that support the organization's Vision, Mission and Objectives. For example, additions and alteration work to cater for the planned future employees' growth, to construct facilities to ready to house new production facilities, etc.

However certain projects may not be obvious to the management that it is in-line with supporting the organisation's core businesses such as green and energy conservation initiatives, implementing intelligent building system, retrofitting facade or roof, etc. Such situations are perfect avenue for FM practitioner to demonstrate to the management their expertise by presenting the potential tangible benefits of such projects to the organisation.

As we have seen severally, to win fund for the projects, FM needs to speak the "number language" of the

Financial Controller and Senior Management, and impress upon that them the business advantage aspect for the proposed FM projects.

In reality, most organizations will use one or more "financial metrics" which they refer to individually or collectively as "ROI". Funding will go first to the proposal that is most likely to provide the best return to the organization. Projects that are not worth the funds invested in them according to the company's criteria will not be funded at all.

Therefore, it is important for FM practitioner to do their numbers before approving the management for fund. If they keep presenting low or negative ROI investment to management, they will lose the management confidence in them as well as respect for their expert advice.

The below explain, with sample calculations, the various financial analysis:

- **Payback or Break Even**

  > Payback = Total Cost / Yearly Revenues

  The amount of time required for the benefits to pay back the cost of the project. The payback period has to be equal or less than the target set by management

  Example:

  The project outlay is $6,000,000.00 and the saving experienced as the result of the new built facilities is $ 1,500,000.00. What is the expected payback period for the project's investment?

  Solution:

  Payback = $ 6,000,000 / $ 1,500,000
  = 4 years

If the organisation's expected payback from any project is less than 5 years, then the above proposed project is viable.

- **Return on Investment (ROI)**

> ROI = Ave Net Revenue/Ave Costs over the PLC

When management asks about the ROI, they are actually asking: "How much will they get back (return) for the money"; "Is it really worthwhile to take the risk (the ROI)?" and "Which project gives the best return for the available fund?".Thus Project's ROI must equal or exceed the ROI (hurdle rate) set by the management.

Example:

The average cost of a 3-year project is estimated to be $3,000,000 per year and the estimated total returns are expected to be $6,000,000.

Solution:

The average return is 6M/3yr = $2M per year

ROI = (Ave Return / Ave Costs) X 100%

    = (2M/3M) X 100%

    = 67%

- **Net Present Value (NPV)**

> NPV = PV (Revenues) – PV (Costs)

The value of future benefits restated in terms of today's money. Decision is based on whether NPV is positive or negative

    NPV > 1, revenues greater than costs

    NPV < 1, revenues less than costs

    NPV = 0, revenue equal costs

A positive result shows that the project is worth pursuing.

Example:

The estimated revenues and costs for the project is as follow:

Year	Revenue	Costs
0	$0	$10,000
1	$12,000	$10,000
2	$16,000	$10,000
3	$20,000	$15,000
4	$40,000	$15,000
5	$60,000	$20,000

Solution:

If the corporate cost of capital is 18%, what is the NPV of your project?

Time Period	Revenue (a)	PV Factor (b)	PV of Revenue (a) x (b)	Costs (c)	PV Factor (d)	PV of Costs (c) x (d)
0	$0	1	$0	$10,000	1	$10,000
1	$12,000	0.8475	$10,169	$10,000	0.8475	$8,475
2	$16,000	0.7182	$11,491	$10,000	0.7182	$7,182
3	$20,000	0.6086	$12,173	$15,000	0.6086	$9,129
4	$40,000	0.5158	$20,632	$15,000	0.5158	$7,737
5	$60,000	0.4371	$26,227	$20,000	0.4371	$8,742
			$80,691			**$51,265**

NPV　　= PV (Revenues) – PV (Costs)

　　　　= 80,691 – 51,265

　　　　= 29,426

NPV is positive. Therefore, pursue with the project

- **Benefit to Cost Ratio (B/C)**

> B/C = PV (Revenues) / PV (Costs)

B/C > 1 : benefits greater than costs

B/C < 1 : benefits less than costs

B/C = 1 : benefits equal cost

Solution:

Based on the above net present value example, what is the B/C ratio of your project?

PV (Revenues) = $ 80,691

PV (Costs)   = $ 51,265

B/C = 80,691 / 51,265

       = 1.57

B/C is preferred by management because a ratio is more meaningful than a pure number. In the examples, NPV is $ 29,426 but it does not show that benefits are over 50% greater than costs, as does the B/C ratio.

Project Selection Techniques Comparison

	Payback	ROI	NPV	B/C
Advantages	• Fast • Simple	• Easily understood and calculated	• Take into consideration the cost of money • Very accurate as compared to other methods	• Take into consideration the cost of money • Very accurate • Easy to interpret ratios than pure numbers
Disadvantages	• Assumes steady revenue • Does not consider the time value of money	• Does not consider the cost of money	• Not easily understood • Cost and revenue not always easy to quantify	• Not easily understood • Cost and revenue not always easy to quantify

15. Communication Strategies

FM has many ways to share and communicate information, reports, events, and so on, whether in person on a one-to-one basis, via written materials and/or a formal presentation, to Management, through staff, or through the e-mail.

The financial, business and leadership aspect of that communication must be delivered in language that the audience and users of the information will understand and will be interested in supporting or acting upon. The aim of communication is to pass across information from a source to a receiver. If the receiver does not understand the language or the technical terms used, then we cannot say that communication has taken place.

> If the receiver does not understand the language or the technical terms used, then communication has failed.

Given the increasing competition for scarce resources both inside and outside of the organization, it is the FM's responsibility to effectively communicate all aspects of an issue to senior management and related department leaders in order to seek their support and help them to make the best decision possible.

Often, the three main areas that need to be emphasized.

i.   Project Goal

Achieving project goal = project support organisation's mission – FM has to emphasize that this project is not just being carried out for the sake of it. The project is to facilitate the realization of the organisation's mission and objective.

Project Goal is to facilitate the realisation of the organisation's mission and objective

Project to meet strategic plans e.g. profitability, market share or technological advance – state expressly how the

State how the project meet the strategic plan of the organisation

project is going to meet the strategic plans of the organization. Many times, senior management doesn't understand the plans that FM want to pursue with the facilities services. For instance, senior management may not really understand why the FM is trying to upgrade facilities to meet the workplace safety and health requirements. So it is left for the FM to communicate these reasons and the consequences of non-compliances.

ii. Project Purpose

Project's outcome must have fitness for use – product or service produced must satisfy real needs – if the project being proposed does not serve a real and perhaps an urgent need of the organization, it might be shelved.

iii. Stakeholder Satisfaction

Project need to satisfies stakeholders' need of intended use

Guidelines on preparing a Proposal for Capital Project

Quantitative Methods – Financial Justifications

- Based on the financial performance analysis, using Payback Period, Net Present Value (NPV), Internal Rate of Return (IRR), Return on Investment (ROI), Cost/Benefit (C/B)
- Based on Facilities-Based Financial Analysis, using Total Cost Analysis and Life Cycle Costing

Qualitative – Non-Financial Justifications

Highlighting that the project:

- Aligns with the corporation's vision & mission
- Supports corporation's business objectives
- Enables improvement and efficiency of business activities
- Is necessary to avoid critical business interruption
- Will yield a high expected ROI
- Will incur minimal financial risk
- Will modernise work processes and result in a cost savings
- Is necessary to ensure compliance with legal / regulatory requirements

Conclusion

Every department in the organisation, including FM, competes for scarce resources. Due to this competition, the "gatekeepers" often have different criteria they use to determine the particular projects that qualify for funding.

FM must conduct a project feasibility study before presenting their proposal to the management. Even though the decision on whether to approve a project or not lies on the shoulders of the management, a proper feasibility study highlight FM's responsibility as a good financial steward – has done his due diligent. It also increase the chance of approval and assured the creditability of the FM's advice.

Bibliography

Cotts, D. G & Rondeau, E. P, 2004, The Facility Manager's Guide to Finance and Budgeting, AMACOM, USA.

Casavant, A. D., 2007, Practical Strategies for Facilities Management, FMS Associates Asia, Singapore.

Ee, S., 2015, Value-Based Facilities Management – How Facilities Practitioners Can Deliver Competitive Advantage to Organisations, Candid Creation, Singapore.

Ee, S., 2018, What is Facilities Management All About? – The Practice of Facilities Management for Today's Dynamic Business Environment, FMSolutions, Singapore.

FMS Associates Asia, 2015, Initiating Facilities Improvements, Singapore.

Resources

Steven Ee has written a number of articles on facilities management which were published in *The Straits Times*. For further reading on value-adding strategies for your facilities practice, download the articles from www.fms-1.com/media, under "Publications".

He also runs FMS Associates Asia, which was founded in 2007 with a mission to increase the recognition of facilities management profession as a value-adding function and business advantage to organisations. FMS Associates Asia offers a series of courses to equip FM practitioners with essential skills to enhance their own performance as well as their organisations'.

FMS Associates Asia Pte Ltd
Website: www.fms-1.com
Email: enquiry@fms-1.com
Telephone: +65 6100 3672

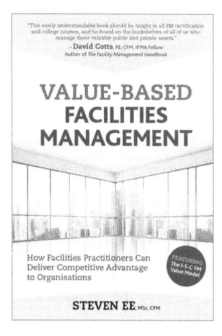

"This easily understandable book should be taught in all FM certification and college courses, and be found on the bookshelves of all of us who manage these valuable public and private assets."

- **David Cotts**, PE, CFM, IFMA Fellow
Author of *The Facility Management Handbook*

VALUE-BASED FACILITIES MANAGEMENT

How Facilities Practitioners Can Deliver Competitive Advantage to Organisations

FEATURING
The I-S-C FM
Value Model

STEVEN EE, MSc, CFM

The discipline of facilities management is often depicted as a support service or technical function, and remains a largely unrecognised profession. Blamed for incurring high maintenance costs or constraining an organisation's performance with a lack of facilities services, the facilities management is beset with a poor self-image. Yet, effective and efficient facilities management can contribute to an organisation's vision of productivity, good repute, and risk management, and play a major role in attracting and retaining talent. What knowledge and skills do you need to be a strategic resource to your company? How do you enable a safe, secure, comfortable, and productive workplace? How do you add value in a way that matters to your organisation? This book answers all these questions and more. This book is intended for easy reading, especially for busy facilities practitioners, to share practical strategies and solutions that facilities management can use to be a business advantage to organisations. It gives you a blueprint to integrate your own value-based facilities management, and become your organisation's valued resource in achieving their bottom line.

Praise for Value-Based Facilities Management

Steven Ee has written a very readable, interesting and important facilities management book that provides thoughtful insights into the role of the facilities professional and how his or her success must be based on knowledge and experience of the business, leadership, stakeholders, resources, as well as on the understanding of key performance indicators, and meeting these requirements. Allowing business management to focus on core business activities provides a key service that facilities management must recognize, and this book provides a detailed guide for its success.

Edmond P. Rondaeu
AIA, CFM, IFMA Fellow

Steven has accurately captured the challenges facing the facilities management community, and offered a viable process for bringing much-needed recognition to the profession through the Identify-Sustain-Contribute Value Model. I look forward to seeing more from Steven as he helps us gain a broader perspective on a crucial function in any organisation that manages a workplace.

Christopher P. Hodges
C.E., CFM, FRICS, IFMA Fellow
Principal, Facility Engineering Associates

Steven Ee's book is unique because first of all it is short and easy to follow. Second, it is a focused study of an important aspect of our profession that is the sustained contribution of facilities management to the corporate mission and company bottom-line by generating VALUE through careful strategic planning and effective operations. Ee's book has laid out the how-to and step-by-step methodology to achieve value creation.

Alex Lam
MRAIC, IFMA Fellow
President, The OCB Network, Toronto Canada

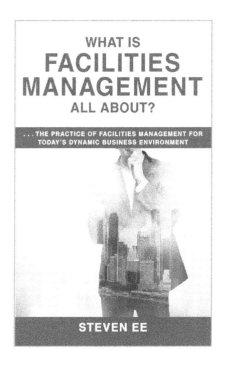

WHAT IS
FACILITIES MANAGEMENT
ALL ABOUT?

...THE PRACTICE OF FACILITIES MANAGEMENT FOR TODAY'S DYNAMIC BUSINESS ENVIRONMENT

STEVEN EE

This book teaches FM practitioners the steps that can help them take decisive steps towards creating clarity and direction in FM.

There is something in this book for both seasoned and new FM practitioners as both face the same problem – their function is viewed as non-strategic, a support role, and a cost centre. As a result of that, many FM practitioners are out of synch with the core business activities of their different organizations and are not fulfilled in their roles. To help them out of their misery, the author shares professional pieces of timely advice to help FM practitioners to not just practice FM the right way, but to also be knowledgeable enough to position their functions as a strategic one.

The book bridges the gap between what is desired in FM and what the reader already knows in a deliberate attempt at offering solutions that cut across the industry.

"What is Facilities Management All About?" tackles the challenges facing FM in a ground-up approach. First, the book seeks to get readers to be aligned with FM identity and proceeds to outline ways in which practitioners can make FM a value centre instead of a cost centre or a profit centre.

At the end of the book, readers will be more informed about the identity of FM, the mission of FM, and the core responsibilities of FM. With this knowledge, they can be in a better position to relate their function to top executives in their organization so as to elevate it to a strategic one. Hence, the book is a must-read for both new and seasoned FM practitioners.

CPSIA information can be obtained
at www.ICGtesting.com
Printed in the USA
BVHW032210271022
650546BV00016B/133